GARDEN OF PLEASURE

YANG CHU'S

GARDEN OF PLEASURE

Edited by

ROSEMARY BRANT

Astrolog Publishing House

Cover Design: Na'ama Yaffe

Production Manager: Dan Gold

P.O. Box 1123, Hod Hasharon 45111, Israel
Tel: 972-9-7412044
Fax: 972-97442714

ISBN 965-494-206-2

Published by Astrolog Publishing House 2005

The Yang Chu chapter of the Lieh Tzu (Book 7)

Originally translated by Anton Forke in 1912

Yang Chu was a classic Chinese philosopher who probably lived in the fourth century BCE. He has been associated with Taoism, although the connection is problematic as the beliefs of Yang Chu are quite different from those of Taoist philosophers such as Chuang-Tzu and Lao Tzu. In ancient times, these thinkers were not considered to be members of the same school of thought. The text attributed to Yang Chu was preserved in the Lieh Tzu, which did not reach its final form until about 400 CE. In it, Yang Chu is not mystical at all. He is mainly concerned with enjoying life to its fullest, with allowing people to express themselves as much as possible, and with not interfering with natural processes.

Contents

Yang Chu's Garden of Pleasure

In ancient Chinese history, the period from 480 to 230 BCE is known as of the period of the Warring States of the Western Chinese Empire. Most Chinese philosophies circulated during this time. Curiously, it is around the same time that the rise of philosophy occurred in Greece, under somewhat similar conditions.

Just as the philosophers in Greece gathered in Athens, the philosophers in ancient China gathered in Liang, the capital of the State of Wei. Among these philosophers were Mencius, one of the greatest supporters of Confucianism, a sort of St. Paul for the movement and Yang Chu's main opponent. Chuang-Tzŭ, a very subtle Taoist sophist came as well. The great statesman and lawmaker Li Kuei arrived, as did Hsün-tzŭ, the philosopher who spoke about original evil. Wênt-zu, the follower of Lao-tzŭ, and Mo-Ti, known for his support of brotherly love, also came. Mo-Ti's name is often cited with Yang Chu's in criticism from Mencius.

Liang attracted a remarkable, perhaps unprecedented, number of original and remarkable thinkers during this period. Eventually, the spread of Christianity in Eastern Europe and Confucianism in China caused this spirit of philosophy to be destroyed or diverted, replacing philosophical thoughts and questions with religion-based rules and rituals.

These philosophies lay hidden for centuries, or were destroyed altogether in the great book burning that took place in 213 BCE. Some philosophies, like Taoism, were altered into codes of belief supported by ritual and worship. Others were preserved only in fragmentary form. The philosophy of Yang Chu falls into the latter category, and a fragment of it was preserved in the Taoist teachings of the Lieh Tzu.

During the golden period of Chinese philosophy, men were occupied with critically examining life. There was a rise in philosophers, who boldly explored the motives and mysteries of existence. These philosophers drew disciples around themselves and traveled from one court to another. They attracted new adherents as they went and argued with rival teachers all over the region on a wide range of issues.

The Court of Liang welcomed these philosophers warmly during the period of about 300 BCE. This was the period in which Yang Chu lived, and the king of Liang treated visiting philosophers very well. He provided them with food and lodgings, and invited anyone who had an interest in pursuing truth and wisdom to his kingdom. It is not clear whether Yang

Garden of Pleasure

Chu was a native of the Wei State, or whether he came, as many other philosophers did, by the lure of having an audience for his thoughts. What is known is that he settled in the area, probably during the reign of King Hwei. A landowner, he stayed in the area until his death in about 250 BCE.

As for his lifestyle, it was probably similar to that of Epicurus, who lived in his famous garden in Athens. Pupils and disciples came to visit Yang Chu, and to hear him discuss his philosophy of pleasure and contentment. Discussions were held in Yang Chu's garden much in the same way they were held in Athenian gardens at the same time. These discussions were memorized and recorded by Meng-sun-Yang, Yang Chu's favorite pupil, and it is thanks to these records that we have the only fragment of Yang Chu's teachings that remain. Although only a fragment, it contains enough details to allow us to form a clear idea of his teaching, and philosophy.

A few details about Yang Chu's personal life can be learned from Chapter 14, a chapter which focuses on an interview between Yang Chu and the King of Liang. In this chapter, Yang Chu discusses the fact that what may be easy and possible for one person can be difficult and impossible for another. Yang Chu goes so far as to suggest that ruling a kingdom is no more difficult than herding a flock of sheep. This chapter reveals that Yang Chu lived the traditional life of a Chinese gentleman. He had a wife, a concubine and a garden. One may even imagine that in this simple and modest environment, he found the pleasure and contentment idealized in his philosophy.

One may learn a few more details about his life from a number of true stories that are contained in the book of Chuang-Tzu and Lieh Tzu. From these, it seems that Yang Chu had a brother named Yang Pu, the hero of a lovely story about a dog who does not recognize his master. It also seems that, like other philosophers of his time, Yang Chu often traveled to other regions with a selection of students, staying at inns, discussing his philosophy in foreign courts, and telling humorous anecdotes about his adventures on the journey. These facts, though few, demonstrate that Yang Chu's life was quite similar to the lives of other major philosophers of his time, both in China and in Greece. They reveal quite a lot about a man who was deep-thinking and cynical, clever and clear-sighted.

It's not surprising that his philosophy did not become widely popular. His ideas were too daring, too revolutionary. Although he probably attracted audiences who were interested in hearing him speak, in his polished and clever manner, about pleasure and fulfilling the senses, most listeners probably left his discussions eager to return to their own rites and rituals, such as worshiping ancestors or nurturing

Taoist superstitions. For unlike those belief systems, there was no place for ritual in Yang Chu's philosophy. He did not allow for a ruling spirit, and had no place for a deity or for inexplicable signs of wonder. For people seeking mysterious secrets such as how to pass through air invisibly, Yang Chu's philosophy would have seemed quite plain. For people seeking life guidance, Yang Chu offered simple happiness, in its most basic form. He criticized things such as self-assertion and self-glorification. With such beliefs, there never could have been many people who followed his philosophies.

In an introduction to the seventh chapter of the Lieh Tzu, the chapter which contains the only fragments of Yang Chu's teachings, Dr. Forke describes his philosophy as a study of scarlet on black. That is to say, scarlet symbolizes the joy of life, and black symbolizes the philosopher's alleged pessimism. While this analogy may seem quite acceptable at first glance, a deeper look reveals it to be quite inaccurate.

One senses the inexplicable insight of the philosopher who so angered Christian commentators, with ideas they considered to be almost poisonous. Yang Chu wasn't interested in things such as virtue and civic duties; he ruled out self-sacrifice, and held things such as goodness, excellence and success in contempt. Instead, he insisted that the purpose of life was individual expression.

Initially, this approach caused Western readers to sense a dark and sinister tone in his teachings, and evoked images of evil spirits from the East. Dr. James Legge, an expert in ancient Chinese philosophy and the author of The Religions of China (1880), described Yang Chu as the "least-erected spirit who ever professed to reason concerning the duties of life and man." As for Yang Chu's teachings, Legge described them as "quite detestable." Frederick Henry Balfour, who also wrote about Oriental studies the late nineteenth century, refers to the "the irreproachable Kuan Chung, who is made to utter the most atrocious doctrines."

Most people who have a preconceived sense of morality will probably agree with the opinions of these two men. For them, philosophers are supposed to view the world from a pristine tower that contains many small windows through which the philosopher looks out. From such a perspective, the philosopher's view of the world should be limited. He should examine the world with detachment and aloofness, perhaps even a little repulsion. In general, philosophical writing contains a sense of coldness and disinterest on behalf of the philosopher. Marcus Aurelius, for example, will always seem a little less than human to most people. Socrates will always seem impossibly stern. Due to these traits, people will always turn to ideal figures such as Christ and Buddha for guidance rather than to philosophers such as Epictetus and Kanada. Thus, while the garden of Epicurus has faded from people's consciousness, the garden of Gethsemane remains vivid, like a picture engraved deeply in people's hearts.

While poets generally belong to a specific location and landscape, philosophers have no country. This is clear in the fragment from Yang Chu that contains the core of his beliefs. In a subtler and more elaborate form, this same idea serves as a basis for Greece's Epicurean philosophy. With calm indifference, Yang Chu achieves the perfection of the ego, similar to that described many centuries later by Max Stirner, a nineteenth century philosopher who wrote the provocative text entitled The Ego and Its Own. In some respects, it is similar to the Charvaka philosophy in India, although Yang Chu's position does not contain the aggressive skepticism that makes the Indian system of beliefs more of a rebellion and less of a philosophy.

Both the Charvaka and the philosophy of Yang Chu encourage man to pursue happiness during his lifetime. However, while studying and nurturing the senses is of utmost importance to Yang Chu, Brihaspati, the Hindu sage who preached the Charvaka throughout his life, is satisfied with creating a formula for pleasure and simply leaving it at that—an empty formula tainted by cynicism and disinterest that is really of little importance to the philosopher himself.

This is expressed in quotations attributed to Brihaspati such as 'Let a man be happy while he lives, and feed on ghee although he runs into debt. When his body is burnt after death, he can never return anyway.'

Yang Chu's philosophy actually goes farther than its Indian counterpart, due to its attention to life, and its intense feelings about it. In some ways, this brings Yang Chu much close to Epicurus, although unlike the Greek philosopher, Yang Chu rejects any notions of life based on semi-moral self-interest, nor does he suggest that there are any philosophic deities. For Yang Chu, man's only purpose is to satisfy his senses during his brief lifetime.

It is this tendency that leads Dr. Forke to suggest that pessimism underlies Yang Chu's philosophy, and provides him with a rationale for saying that Yang Chu's view of life is black, and the moments of pleasure appear as splashes of scarlet. But the pessimism that Dr. Forke senses is not really there. It only appears in examples Yang Chu presents of how ridiculous it is to pursue fame, and in discussions of how man obstructs his own path toward happiness. Not only is pessimism absent from Yang Chu's philosophy—his approach to life is actually in direct opposition to it.

It's true that Yang Chu talks about how short life is, and that there is no such thing as an afterlife.

Garden of Pleasure

It's also true that he criticizes virtues, and the obstructions they cause in fully sensing and enjoying life. However, in no way does this position create or support a pessimistic view of life. To the contrary, Yang Chu has a very deep value for life, clearly believing that many of the things that are widely believed to be praiseworthy are, in fact, useless. A philosopher who believes that satisfying a man's senses is the most important thing in life could not possibly be pessimistic. This would negate his own philosophy.

The main principle of Yang Chu's philosophy is that both life and death should be disregarded. That is to say, both life and death exist, and that is fine. The best should be extracted from each of these things. Things such as struggle, the inability to be satisfied, greed, worry, fame, and false pursuit of virtue should be avoided. Such things are not only unnecessary, they also disturb the soul.

The only gift man really has is himself, and his sense of self. That is all he is born with, and it dies when he dies. It is man's responsibility to preserve this gift throughout his life, until the moment of death. He shouldn't try to attain more than his life, nor should he try to reject it. He should simply accept it as it is.

All things that help the individual to develop are positive. All things that distort or obstruct the individual are negative. Things that fall in the latter category include virtue, the desire to become famous and powerful, and the quest to control the lives of other people. Altering one's own behavior in order to conform to the expectations of other people is also a negative influence in life.

When these negative influences control people, it leads them to unhappiness. They live their lives in a state of sickness. Their personalities become deformed and destroyed, or they simply become miserable and unhappy. They pursue things that are impossible to achieve, and ignore the potential for happiness that lies at their doorstep. They collapse in exhaustion, die, and are forgotten.

Simple pleasures such as the clear light of day do not bring them any happiness. Indeed, the very word pleasure has no meaning for them, and their life is filled with nothing but restlessness, worry, and unhappiness. It is only natural that people have individual desires and cravings. After all, it is in these desires that a person's individuality resides. Yang Chu sees life as it is, without fear and without interest. He follows his own path, and stays true to himself. He doesn't worry. He knows that even simple things will bring him pleasure, because experiencing pleasure is the main principle of his belief system. He depends only upon his senses and through this focus, learns to understand them. When he ages and his senses begin to deteriorate, he rejects life, because it has no more use for him. Like the wise man of Wei, he enters nothingness.

Yang Chu explains his doctrine on the fulfillment of the senses, in a calm, careless, and relaxed manner. There is no pessimism in his philosophy. There may be similarities between his ideas and those of naturalism, that rejects any notion of the supernatural, and sensualism, that finds feelings to be the only criterion for what is good. Pessimism, however, has little in common with Yang Chu's philosophy. Most religions which view natural desires as a legacy of nature and a sign of original and natural evil have pessimism at their base. Yang Chu had nothing in common with these religions, as he urged people to follow their natural desires and inclinations, regardless of where they may lead.

From this, one may find the answer to a riddle that has puzzled students of Lieh Tzu, Taoism's great representative, for years. Why is this text, the only fragment of Yang Chu's thoughts, preserved in the book of Lieh Tzu?

Taoism is based on naturalism. Its main message to students is to follow and obey the laws of nature. Both Yang Chu and Lieh Tzu begin at the same starting point—a close examination of nature. In both their opinions, existence is natural. In itself, it is neither good nor bad. For both of these philosophers, morality based on social conventions is problematic.

"The perfect man is he who regards the body, and the things of the universe, as belonging to the universe," says Yang Chu.

This statement conveys an idea of unity with nature and freedom that is equally true for Taoism. With such similarities, it is hard to believe there could be major contradictions—even conflicts—between the two philosophies. However, the Taoist idea that all things belong to the universe, that all things are common property, and that anything that is taken is therefore stolen from the universe, is distinct to Taoism, and has no place in Yang Chu's philosophy.

Lieh Tzu says that people steal their existence from nature through unconscious theft. This is also a Taoist doctrine. So is the belief that desires and cravings should be kept to a minimum and, if possible, ignored.

In Chapter 2 of Lieh Tzu's book, it is written: "They followed their natural instincts, feeling neither joy in life, nor abhorrence of death. Thus they came to no untimely ends."

This can be compared to the following statement from Yang Chu:

"Once you have acquired life, do not pay any attention to it and simply allow it to occur. Take note of its desires and wishes, and in this manner wait for death."

Perhaps the best comparison of the two philosophers is as follows: Yang Chu is the young naturalist philosopher, and Lieh Tzu is the elderly one. Of course, it is possible that further material connecting Yang Chu's beliefs to those of the Taoists, material that would explain why an excerpt of his teachings appears in the book of Lieh Tzu, has simply been lost.

The difference between the two philosophers is most apparent in their divergent perspectives on behavior. Their similarity is based on that single sentence, noted previously, in which Yang Chu discusses the unity and freedom between man and nature. That is the only metaphysical speculation to be found in the fragment from Yang Chu. It may be an exception to the doctrine generally expounded in his writing, or it may be a hint as to why his writing is included at all in the text of Lieh Tzu. Certainly, the presence of the Yang Chu chapter is a question that has puzzled students of Taoism for years.

Most of Yang Chu's work concerns itself with how one should behave, and in this he is markedly different from Lieh Tzu. Both believed that life and nature were natural events that were governed by laws that could not be changed by humans. However, from this common base they drew quite different conclusions about how one should live one's life.

Yang Chu felt life was controlled by the senses. His philosophy was based on the senses, and on the belief that man should live in harmony with his senses by giving in to their desires and by striving for nothing other than sensual fulfillment. According to Yang Chu, every action a person takes should be guided by his senses. Nature, in itself, is good. Man becomes bad when he turns away from nature, when his behavior conflicts with nature, when he tries to live according to a morality that opposes nature, when he strives to collect wealth, or when he limits or obstruct his own senses.

From this perspective, Yang Chu builds a philosophy in which life is logical, and not at all moral. A man's purpose in life is to nurture the senses. His ultimate goal is to fulfill sensual desires. This much is obvious, and even if we suspect some deeper metaphysical message elsewhere in his teachings, we cannot pretend that Yang Chu does not believe man should satisfy his senses. Even Epicurus seems wishy-washy in this respect when compared to the certainty of Yang Chu. Yang Chu does not refer to philosophical pleasures, either; he refers to real, tangible pleasures. According to him, all sensual pleasures are good. None are bad.

"Allow the ear to hear what it likes to hear, and the eye to see what it enjoys. Allow the nose to smell what it likes, and the mouth to say what it wants. Allow the body to enjoy the comforts it likes to have, and the mind to do what it likes."

Logically, philosophy that claims to be based on the individual must be based on an examination of the individual's senses. Furthermore, even if study of the senses isn't the basis for philosophy today, it is certainly the basis for modern human actions. Increasingly, study of the senses is gaining interest from people searching for improved self-expression.

Although they start from the same basis, the Taoist philosopher turns away from the sensual and physical, and explores the intangible and unknowable. For the Taoist who is ultimately concerned with metaphysics, life is strange, motionless, and passive. It is also rich, resistant, and intangible. The Taoist urges his students to seek out an understanding of the mysterious force that is ultimately the source of all natural phenomena. He teaches students to learn the ways of nature, instructing them on how to let oneself drift and become one with nature. Satisfying desire has no part in this philosophy.

Lieh Tzu says people who are exceptionally beautiful become vain. People who are exceptionally strong become violent. According to Lieh Tzu, such people cannot be instructed in the ways of Tao. Young people are incapable of speaking about Tao correctly; clearly, they cannot live according to Tao philosophy.

This issue marks the clear division between the two philosophers. For Yang Chu, satisfying the senses is of utmost importance. In youth, one can fully satisfy the sense. With age comes restraint and the inability—and ultimate rejection—of fulfilling the senses. By contrast, restraint and renunciation are necessary from the start for Lieh Tzu. Otherwise, one cannot proceed with Taoism. Youth can only pursue the way of Tao if it opposes its natural instincts.

Lieh Tzu promotes passivity, old age, and introspection. Yang Chu advocates joy and happiness.

The latter's philosophy is based on happiness that is easy to achieve. It must be attainable and handy, free of things such as hard, unpleasant work that numbs the senses and turns humans into beasts. Even wealth is not favored by Yang Chu, as it is seen as a burden that restricts the individual.

"Yuan Hsie lived in Lu and was poor. Tse Kung lived in Wei and was wealthy.

"One was bothered by poverty. The other was worried by his wealth.

"So, neither poverty nor wealth is good.

"Enjoy life and live at ease. People who know how to enjoy life are not poor. People who live at ease do not need great wealth."

Yang Chu does not explain how one is supposed to enjoy life and life at ease. Maybe for him, the ability to enjoy life came naturally when he discovered that pursuing wealth would not bring happiness. His writings do not contain any indication that he supported socialism, nor did he feel that an individual's actions should be limited by some more powerful being. To the contrary, he was totally individualistic and opposed to authority. He imagines an idyllic world, something that may have existed in the distant past, when no one fought to achieve power over others, and no one was interested in empty concepts such as fame. In such a world, the only important thing is living life—no matter how short—in a manner that brings happiness to the individual. He contrasts life in the past with the current way of living, when issues such as struggle, control, and wealth have turned humans into miserable slaves. According to Yang Chu:

"The Ancients knew that life is short, and that all creatures die suddenly. Thanks to this knowledge, they gave in to their impulses and natural inclinations.

"They didn't deny themselves anything that could give them pleasure. They didn't seek out fame, but followed their own natures. They went along with their desires, and never restricted their inclinations. They did not seek fame after death. They didn't do anything criminal either. They paid no attention to things like glory, fame, status and position, and paid no attention to how long they lived."

Unlike other theories, Yang Chu's philosophy truly promotes the individual. Other philosophies of the time only pretended to promote the individual; those doctrines actually caused people to suffer and work. In those philosophies, ideas of egoism overstepped the limits of truly nurturing the self. Instead, and for selfish, vain, often petty reasons, they sought to control others and impose upon them terms of slavery and destitution. These philosophies ultimately sought to limit and destroy individuality, thereby confining individuals into a type of slavery.

A British writer from the early twentieth century wrote the following: "Selfishness is not living as one wishes to live, it is asking others to live as one wishes to live. And unselfishness is letting other people's lives alone, not interfering with them."

According to this definition, selfishness is the result of stupid and unreasonable vanity. True egoism has nothing in common with selfishness. Actually, it is completely unselfish, as a true egoist is satisfied with simply living his own life. He will help or assist others when necessary, but being involved with others' lives is not necessary for him to live his own life.

This perspective is described in the following words from Yang Chu:

"So, we can cure the ill and feed the hungry. We can provide warmth to those who are cold, and help people who are suffering." However, as individuals we must be happy to live own lives, and to discover what means of expression bring us fulfillment.

For Yang Chu, whether this ultimate expression of individuality is considered moral or immoral is completely irrelevant. He writes in a calm and unemotional manner, demonstrating a quiet nature and conveying the sense that he has attained the contentment and harmony he promotes. In the pamphlet Les Théories Individualistes Chinoises, Alexandra David writes about this unusually simple style, what she describes as "la singulière simplicité d'expression de ce 'négateur du sacre.'" She says his teachings are essentially quiet, deeply intelligent and indifferent. Yang Chu does not encourage a specific path or behavior. What may bring pleasure to one person may seem ridiculous to another. As long as a person expresses his true desires, the form that expression takes is only important to him. What others think about it is totally irrelevant. Things such as pleasure and happiness are completely relative. For the old farmer in Sung, the warm sun on his naked back brings pleasure. For Tse Chan's indulgent brothers, drinking fine wine and wooing exceptionally beautiful women brings pleasure. Tuan-Mu-Shu wanders in the wonderful pavilions in Wei, counting the last days of his youth in which he can enjoy songs and happiness. A peasant in Sung is delighted by plain food that tastes terrible to another person. Although we may tell people about our pleasures, we cannot force our pleasures upon others.

Wealth may increase a person's desire, but it cannot increase happiness. In fact, wealth may even reduce happiness. The only things that really matter are those things that are necessary for life. Lacking those essentials makes life worthless.

"If man could live without clothes and food, there would be no need for rulers or being ruled."

The struggle, often useless, for a plain life restricts a person's ability to nurture their own personality. This hardens the personality in such a way that it is no longer worth nurturing.

One can criticize or even hate a person who indulges in his own sensual pleasures—that is question of taste. However, regardless of whether such a person is gross or crude, one must recognize that he has tried to express his individuality, attempted to achieve something which, to him, seems worth achieving. By contrast, a person who has no individuality left, who has nothing distinct to express, has lost the only thing in life that had value. It doesn't matter whether failure or success led to such a state, the person himself cannot be saved. Even thinking about such a person is a waste of time. Rich or poor, he is already dead, and can be of no use to anyone at all. Indeed, he may only be a hindrance.

Such people have deserted life. Whether they live or die doesn't really matter. They have allowed themselves to be controlled by external rather than internal factors.

"They are urged forward by fame and pushed backwards by laws. They are almost always anxious... They squander the happiest moments of the present, and cannot even experience those feelings for one hour."

Regarding the issue of self-sacrifice, Yang Chu is unambiguous. Life is only important to the person who lives it. Even then, it is only important while it is being lived. The only thing that can be achieved through self-sacrifice is, perhaps, a little fame. If fame has any negative effect on the personality, it is wrong. If a man wants to give away things that are not necessary for his life, that is fine. However, his own life is precious. To harm one's own life in order to achieve fame, because others think it is the right thing to do or because it is expected, is wrong. If the world expects self-sacrifice, the world is wrong and the situation that calls for this self-sacrifice is wrong.

Chapter 12 is devoted to this issue, and has been criticized widely. In this chapter, Yang Chu presents an extreme case in which the wise man faces the universe. Most of the chapter is concerned with justifying Yang Chu's radical perspective on self-sacrifice.

Yang Chu refers to the idyllic past he imagines: "If the Ancients could have helped the world by hurting a hair on their own heads, they would not have done it. And, if the universe had been offered to a single person, he would not have accepted it.

"Because nobody would damage a single hair, and because nobody would do anything to help the world, the world was in a perfect state."

Self-sacrifice is the result of a wrong and unbalanced condition of life. If fame and self-glorification at the expense of others did not exist, self-sacrifice would be unnecessary.

If everyone was happy and satisfied, self-sacrifice and self-aggrandizement would be unnecessary. If humanity believes self-sacrifice is desirable, then it is because people believe in false egoism. If this is the case, vanity and ignorance have led humanity to a point in which accepted morals are unreasonable and unnecessary.

This is an important observation, because a superficial reading of this chapter can be quite misleading. Indeed, such readings have led many critics to feel a sense of anger at Yang Chu. While such anger may be justified according to current ideas of what is moral, it is quite out of place in an examination of the philosopher himself.

According to Yang Chu, taking care of oneself and expressing one's own personality is every man's primary duty. This is his natural purpose. When this purpose meets with interference, for example, when it is distorted or unfulfilled, an environment

Garden of Pleasure

is created in which things such as injustice, greed, and vanity may prosper. If mankind fulfilled his own desires, he would never encounter these unnecessary evils. Furthermore, these problems demand solutions that are similarly unnecessary. Thus, things known as virtues are actually solutions that were created to solve the problem of vices that should never have been created in the first place.

The rest of Chapter 12 contains an analysis of the various degrees of self-sacrifice. Although this may be interesting from a logical point of view, it is not terribly significant. As in Chapter 9, the chapter which discusses the happily indulgent brothers, Yang Chu states an extreme case and leaves the task of qualification to his students.

Chapters 3, 4, 8, 11, 13 and 15 contain a description of how to live according to a doctrine of materialism, a set of beliefs in which only matter exists, and in which consciousness and will are due totally to material agency. According to this philosophy, there is no mystery about life. It is natural and unavoidable. Materialism is simply a fact of life.

Regardless of whether we are good or bad, moral or immoral, we all share the same fate: we live, we die, and then we are forgotten.

Our personality dies with us, regardless of whether we were virtuous or villainous, regardless of whether we accept death calmly, or fight it to the end. The fate that awaits the body of a saint is the same fate that awaits the body of a thief.

Modern readers may accept or deny this statement, but it should be noted that early Taoists, Confucians, and Buddhists did not believe in a conscious after-life. Like Yang Chu, they assumed that the end of life was final and unavoidable. In this manner, Yang Chu was not actually refuting any of the common beliefs of his time. Philosophy that is based on deduction must deal with facts; as a result, such philosophies are limited by those facts. Even if man, according to Taoism, is the highest evolved form in nature, his fate is bounded by his life.

Nothing is known about what exists, if anything, beyond life. If we had proof of anything beyond life, there would be no need for things such as philosophy, speculation, perhaps even religion. One may theorize about the motive for life, but all guesses are just that—guesses. The philosopher who knows only what can be known tries to present existence as something that can be a little happier, more certain, more worthy of wanting to live. This is, after all, the main instinct of animals and men.

If a person has glimpsed out of the windows of the tower of philosophy, it doesn't really matter how he chooses to pursue his life. He may pursue happiness or self-sacrifice; he may pursue sadness or the power that comes with importance; he may also immerse

Garden of Pleasure

himself, as in the Tao ideal, in a quiet and reflective life. Whatever his choice, as long as he has peered through the windows of philosophical inquiries, he has seen a land where better, finer, less miserable things are being done. In that land, the harshness and struggle of life may seem like the distant echo of an old record that doesn't sound right anymore, or a fog that lifts suddenly, and takes man's vain pursuits and unhappiness with it.

More knowledge about life cannot be gained through philosophy. However, philosophy can change how life is known. Life remains the same, no matter how we view it. Yang Chu is not interested in speculation; he knows certain things will always be unknowable. Instead, he is concerned with guiding man to a Utopia in which he can live his life in happiness and prepare for death without complaining.

Once he has declared that life does not last forever, Yang Chu turns his attention to considering what it is that makes men most happy during their lives. This is the strength in his teachings. If happiness is gained only by fulfilling the senses, it follows that people should nurture the senses in order to achieve happiness easily and perfectly. A sense for beauty will take the place of vanity and aggression, because through guidance of his senses, man will realize that he must desire what is beautiful. First, he will want what is necessary; then he will desire what is comfortable; finally, he will want what is beautiful. Cultivating the senses is never shameful. Man is only ashamed when he stunts or limits his senses.

Common people require common pleasures. These can always be found, often too easily. For example, Yang Chu does not say that drinking alcohol is a good or desirable thing, nor does he say that excessive desire for women is admirable. However, he does say that any inclination, regardless of whether it is crude, disgusting or even indefensible, is better than the desire to rule and control others. A man who overindulges his own senses may ruin his own health. A man who desires power and authority can ruin the life of a whole nation.

If society pursues and nurtures happiness, it will raise the ideal of pleasure among its people. Such a society will reveal the torment that lies in pursuits of wealth, flashy displays, drunken parties, inflated self-worth achieved at the expense of others, aggression, greed, vanity, and insatiability. These negative tendencies, barely perceived in societies that value virtues, will be seen as they truly exist. People will realize that happiness is simple to achieve. They will learn about their senses, understand them a little, and realizes that each person can find happiness easily, through his own means, and in his own way.

This is the materialist Utopia. It is Yang Chu's philosophy.

Aside from the chapter in the book of Lieh Tzu, there seem to be a few stories about Yang Chu and his teachings in other parts of the book of Lieh Tzu, and in the book of Chuang-Tzu. For the most part, these have been included in other works on the Taoist philosophers, and are not included here.

The exception to this is the following anecdote, which shows the happy skepticism of Yang Chu, who believed that the only certain thing in life was death. The story goes like this:

Yang Chu's neighbor lost a sheep.

The neighbor began looking for the sheep with all of his relatives Then he asked Yang Chu's servants to help as well.

"Why do you need so many people to help you find a single lost sheep?" asked Yang Chu in astonishment

"There are many paths we must follow," said the neighbor.

When the neighbor returned, Yang Chu asked if he had found the sheep. The neighbor said he had given up the search, and Yang Chu asked why.

 "There were many forks in the paths," explained his neighbor. "I didn't know which to choose, so I simply stopped searching."

Yang Chu became very thoughtful. For a full day, he neither spoke nor smiled. His disciples were surprised by his behavior. "A sheep is not very valuable," they said. "And it wasn't your sheep anyway. So why is this lost sheep making you so unhappy?"

Yang Chu didn't answer.

His students couldn't understand why Yang Chu was silent, and Meng-sun-Yang talked to Hsin-tu-tse about it.

Another day, Hsin-tu-tse and Meng-sun-Yang approached Yang Chu.

"Three brothers traveled through the provinces of Chi and Lu," they said. "They had studied humanity and justice under the same teacher.

"When they came to their father's house, their father asked them to tell him the final conclusion of their studies.

"The first son said: 'Studying humanity and justice has taught me to love and respect my body, and not value fame and glory too much.'

"The second son said: 'Studying humanity and justice has taught me to sacrifice my body in order to obtain fame and glory.'

"The third son said: 'Studying humanity and justice has taught me to seek a way of appeasing the desires of my body and the desire for fame.'

"These three theories are contradictory, but they come from learning under the same teacher. Which of them is true? Which of them is false?"

Yang Chu answered:

"There was once a man who lived by a river. He knew all there was to know about the river, and was an excellent swimmer. He earned his living by driving a boat, and was quite rich from this occupation. Indeed, he was wealthy enough to support a hundred people.

"Many people came to this man to learn how to swim. They brought him a bag of grain in payment to become his students.

"About half of these students drowned.

"When they came to him, they wanted to swim, not drown. About half of his students succeeded and half of them failed. That is, half learnt to swim, and half drowned.

"Which of the students were right? Which of the students were wrong?"

Hsin-tu-tse didn't say anything. Meng-sun-Yang turned to Hsin-tu-tse and said:

"Well? Isn't this right? Your question was vague, so the Master's answer is vague too. Now, I am even more confused than I was before!"

Hsin-tu-tse answered:

"The sheep was lost because large roads are split into many small paths.

"When there are many paths in wisdom, many students get lost. It doesn't matter if all students begin at the same starting point, there are many divergent paths at the end.

"The only thing that restores equality is death, and the end of the personality that comes with death.

"It is unfortunate that, as a longtime student of the Master and his philosophy, you don't understand his parables."

Using his own unique grace, charm and humor, Yang Chu points out that though all philosophies may begin at the same place, everything else depends upon personality. From the single truth of life, an infinite number of deductions may be reached, all of which are conflicting and opposing, false and true.

After all the conversations, discussions, and philosophical debates, the only thing that is really a fact is that humans live and die. How we live—whether in comfort or discomfort, whether we are good or bad, whether we are happy or happy, whether we seek wisdom or momentary pleasures—is totally unimportant. In the end, we die and are forgotten.

At best, we may look back with regret on the few happy days we enjoyed. Maybe our memories will help us recall temporary happiness. In essence, these are the only things that life really gives us, these memories that are hidden in the treasure chest of our lives, the only true expression of personality that fate and selfishness allows.

The sheep that Yang Chu's neighbor lost is still lost, wandering along the various conflicting paths of philosophical thought and wisdom. Life is a simple thing that man has made complicated. The goal of life is to achieve happiness, but happiness is different for every person.

In our own hearts, we know that we have felt happiness and that our lives are oriented toward happiness. Here, Yang Chu reminds us of death. He says life would be happy if men were interested in making life happy. If life is unhappy, it is because men are seeking other things, and this makes their lives unhappy.

Men would be happy if they were content to pursue only the happiness of satisfying their senses. Why do men fight, rob, kill and hurt? Is this left over from some ancient tradition of killing, stealing land, and searching for power? Is this what remains of a time when the only means of expression was through violence? For Yang Chu, the pursuit of simple, deep, and individual happiness is the goal that men should pursue. First, however, they must remove the shackles of pride and arrogance, and stop fooling themselves. The best thing life can offer is happiness. Death, after all, is inevitable. No philosopher, no matter how spiritual, can alter this fact of life.

Happiness from simple pleasures, and death as the end of everything, is the basis of Yang Chu's philosophy. Life is unavoidable and so is death. Wisdom is relative, and the pursuit of wisdom cannot stop death. People must achieve their own happiness during life. Nothing else, neither wisdom nor virtue, nor cruelty nor benefiting from others, can help. Every one must pursue happiness as an individual. It is hard to express this happiness, and even more difficult to share it. The final solution for happiness must come from you and must be enough for you.

YANG CHU'S GARDEN OF PLEASURE

The Yang Chu chapter
of the Lieh Tzu, Book 7

Chapter 1

The Vanity of Fame

While traveling in Lu, Yang Chu stayed with Meng-sun-Yang.

"A man can never be more than man," said Meng, "so why do people try to be famous?"

"If they want to be famous," said Yang Chu, "it is because they want to be rich."

"Then why aren't they satisfied when they become rich?" Meng asked.

"Because they want to be honored as well," said Yang Chu.

"Then why don't they stop once they are honored?" asked Meng.

"Because of their mortality," said Yang Chu.

"But what can they want after they die?" asked Meng.

"They think of their offspring, of the generations to come," said Yang Chu.

"And how can their fame be available to their offspring?" asked Meng.

To this, Yang Chu answered: "People go through

physical and mental hardships in order to be famous. They get ride of their glory to benefit their family and friends. Their neighbors and acquaintances benefit too. Imagine how much more their offspring benefit. Nevertheless, it is typical of people who want real fame to neglect themselves. They don't pay attention to their personal needs and this leads to poverty. In the same manner, they may become unpretentious, and this is like being modest."

Considering all of this, how can fame be ignored? How can fame occur naturally?

The ignorant give up reality in their pursuit of fame. By doing this, they will be disappointed that nothing can save them from danger and death, and not only learn how to distinguish between ease and pleasure, and between sorrow and grief.

Chapter 2

Real and False Greatness

Yang Chu said:

"When Kuan Ching[1] was a minister for the King of Ch'i, he behaved in the following manner. When the king acted without restraint, Kuan Ching was unrestrained as well. When the king behaved recklessly, Kuan Ching was reckless too. Kuan obeyed the king and fulfilled his every wish. In this manner, he helped the kingdom to prosper. However, when the king died, Kuan Ching was simply Mr. Kuan again—nothing more.

"When Tien[2] was a minister for the King of Ch'i, he behaved in the following manner. When the king was overpowering and repressive, Tien showed courtesy and compassion. When the king collected taxes, Tien distributed money. The people admired Tien for these actions. He eventually became the King of Ch'i, and his offspring rule it to this day.

"If anybody is truly great, he is poor. If anyone's greatness is false, he is rich."

Yang Chu said:

"The man who is truly good is not famous. If he is famous, he is not really a good man, as fame is nothing but falsehood.

"In ancient times, Yao and Shun pretended to give up their empire to Hsu-yu and Shan-Chuan. However, they didn't actually give up the empire, and enjoyed happiness for a hundred years.

"Po Yo and Shu-Ch'i[3] really did give up their empire. These sons of Prince Ku-Chu lost their kingdom because of their father's request, and died of starvation on the mountain of Shou-Yang.

"This is the difference between the truth and falseness."

Chapter 3

The Shortness of Conscious Life

Yang Chu said:

"One hundred years is considered to be a long life, but only one in one thousand people live this long. However, even those that live this long spend many years—about half of the time—in the unconsciousness of infancy and old age.

"The time that passes while sleeping at night, and the time wasted during the day, amount to another half of one's life. Pain, sickness, sorrow, and fear fill up another half of the time. Ultimately, a person who lives a long life really only has ten years of enjoyment. And even then, not a single hour is free from some anxiety or another.

"What is the purpose of life, then? What makes it pleasant? Comfort and elegance, music and beauty. Still, one cannot always fulfill one's desire for comfort and elegance, nor can one constantly enjoy beauty and music.

"Furthermore, people are always being warned by punishments and encouraged by rewards. They are urged forward by fame and pushed backwards by laws. They are almost always anxious. They strive to achieve one vain hour of glory, to leave a legacy that will continue after their death. In these efforts, they walk down solitary paths, analyzing everything that they see and hear, carefully considering what is good for their body and mind. They squander the happiest moments of the present, and cannot even experience these feelings for one hour.

"How are free people really any different from chained criminals?

"The Ancients knew that life is short, and that all creatures die suddenly. Thanks to this knowledge, they gave in to their impulses and natural inclinations.

"They didn't deny themselves anything that could give them pleasure. They didn't seek out fame, but followed their own nature. They went along with their desires, and never restricted their inclinations. They did not seek fame after death. They didn't do anything criminal either. They paid no attention to things like glory, fame, status and position, and paid no attention to how long they lived."

Chapter 4

Death the Equalizer

Yang Chu said:

"In life, all living things are different. In death, all living things are alike.

"In life, there is a difference between intelligence and stupidity, between being honored and being looked down upon. In death, there is equality in rottenness and decay. Neither can be prevented. Although intelligence, stupidity, reverence, and condescension exist, they cannot be affected by humans, just as rottenness and decay cannot be prevented. Humans cannot make life and death. They cannot make intelligence, stupidity, reverence or lowness. All beings live and die equally. All are equally wise and stupid, honorable and disrespected.

"Some people die at the age of ten; others live to be one hundred years old. Still, the wise and the kindhearted die, just as the feeble-minded and cruel die.

"Living, they were known as Yao and Shun[4]. Dead,

they are an indistinguishable pile of bones. But if we concentrate on enjoying life, we will have no time to worry about what comes after death."

Chapter 5

False Virtues

Yang Chu said:

"Po Yi did not live without desire. He was so proud of his pure mind that he didn't eat and, as a consequence, died of starvation.

"Chan Chi[5] did not live without passion. He was so proud of his virtue that he failed to produce offspring.

"People who pursue purity and virtue and, as a result, behave falsely, are like these men."

Chapter 6

The Ideal Life

Yang Chu said:

"Yuan Hsie lived in Lu and was poor. Tse Kung[6] lived in Wei and was wealthy.

"One was bothered by poverty. The other was worried because of his wealth.

"So, neither poverty nor wealth is good.

"In that case, what should a person do?

"My answer is this: Enjoy life and live at ease. People who know how to enjoy life are not poor. People who live at ease do not need great wealth."

Chapter 7

Duty to the Living and the Dead

Yang Chu said:

"There is an old saying which goes like this: We should pity the living and part with the dead. It is a wise saying.

"Pity is not just a passing feeling.

"So, we can cure the ill and feed the hungry. We can provide warmth to those who are cold, and help people who are suffering. However, as for the dead, once we have mourned them properly, there is no point in putting valuables in their graves, or dressing them in fine clothing, or offering sacrifices in their honor, or creating images in their likeness.

Chapter 8

The Art of Life

Yen-Ping-Chung asked Kuan-Yi-Wu[7] about cherishing life.

Kuan-Yi-Wu answered:

"To cherish life is to simply let it run its course, without impeding or blocking it."

"What do you mean?" asked Yen-Ping-Chung.

"Allow the ear to hear what it likes to hear," answered Kuan-Yi-Wu, "and the eye to see what it enjoys. Allow the nose to smell what it likes, and the mouth to say what it wants. Allow the body to enjoy the comforts it likes to have, and the mind to do what it likes.

"The ear likes to hear music. If the ear is not allowed to hear music, it is an obstacle to hearing.

"The eye likes to see beauty. If the eye is not allowed to see beauty, it is an obstacle to seeing.

"The nose likes to smell perfume. If the nose is not allowed to smell perfume, it is an obstacle to smelling.

"The mouth likes to talk about what is right and what is wrong. If the mouth is not allowed to speak, it is an obstacle to understanding.

"The body enjoys things such as rich foods and fine clothing. If a body is not permitted to have these comforts, it is an obstacle to the body's senses.

"The mind likes to be at peace. If the mind is not allowed to rest, it is an obstacle to the mind's nature.

"All these obstacle cause anxiety and agitation.

"Nurturing these obstacles that cause anxiety is like a sickness. One is unable to get rid of these barriers, and so although one may have a long life, it will be a sad life. Preserving life so that it is one hundred, one thousand, even ten thousand years long, is not what I call cherishing life.

"I understand that to take pleasure in life is to live in calm enjoyment. It is to live without trying to obstruct the senses. It is to wait for death calmly—for a day, a month, a year or even ten years.

"I have told you about how to cherish life," said Kuan-Yi-Wu. "Now, please tell me about burying the dead."

"Burying the dead is not very important," said Yen-Ping-Chung. "What should I tell you about it?"

"I really want to hear it," replied Kuan-Yi-Wu.

Yen-Ping-Chung answered:

"What can I do when I am dead? They may burn my body or throw it into deep water. They may bury my body or leave it unburied. They may wrap my body in a cloth and throw it into a ditch or cover it with fine clothes and place it in an elaborate stone coffin. All of these possibilities depend on mere chance."

Kuan-Yi-Wu looked at Pao-Shu-huang-tse. "We have both made some progress in the doctrine of life and death," he said.

Chapter 9

The Happy Hedonists

Tse-Chan[8] was a minister in Cheng. He governed for three years, and governed well. Good people obeyed his orders, and bad people were fearful of his laws. Cheng was governed in this manner, and the princes were afraid of it.

Tse-Chan had an elder brother named Kung-sun-Chow, and a younger brother named Kung-sun-Mu. The elder brother loved to eat and the younger brother loved women.

At Kung-sun-Chow's house, a thousand barrels of wine were stored, and there were heaps of yeast as well. The stench of drugs and liquor could be smelled a hundred feet from the door of the house, offending neighbors and people passing by.

Kung-sun-Chow was drunk so often that he had no feelings of regret or sorrow. He had no idea of what was safe or dangerous in life. He didn't even know what was going on in his own house, and was unaware if something was present or missing.

He knew nothing about the lives of his close or distant relatives[9], and didn't even know if someone had been born or died.

He was so oblivious to his surroundings that water, fire, or even swords could almost touch him without him being aware of it.

At Kung-sun-Mu's house, there was a compound of about thirty or forty apartments to house beautiful women. Kung-sun-Mu was so captivated by the charms of women that he neglected relatives and friends, and paid no attention to his family. He spent all of his time in his inner courtyard, turning nighttime into day.

Over the course of three months, he left his compound only once, and still, he felt unsatisfied.

If there was a pretty girl in the neighborhood, he would do anything to win her heart. He would bribe her and flatter her ceaselessly, stopping only if it was truly impossible to attain what he wanted.

Tse-Chan thought these things over, and secretly went to consult with Teng-hsi.

"I have heard that how one cares for oneself influences one's family," said Tse-Chan, "and that how one cares for one's family influences the state. In other words, by paying attention to the things closest to home, one affects things that are more distant. I have taken care of my kingdom, and it is in good shape, but my family is in disorder. Perhaps this is not the right way. What should I do? How can I help my brothers?"

"I have thought about this issue for a long time," said Teng-hsi, "but dared not approach you first. Why don't you use your power to control them? Encourage them by telling them about the importance of life and nature; rebuke them gently by telling them about the benefits of virtuous and appropriate behavior."

Tse-Chan followed Teng-hsi's advice. When he next saw his brothers, he said to them:

"The ability to think is what makes man superior to animals and birds," he said. "By using his mind, man understands virtue and morality, modesty and appropriate behavior. This is the behavior that helps him to achieve glory and success. You, however, are only interested in things that excite your senses. You indulge in your wicked desires, thereby endangering your lives and natures.

"Listen to what I say. Repent in the morning, and

by evening you will have already improved your lives."

Chow and Mu said:

"We knew all of this a long time ago, and made our decision from choice.

"We didn't need your advice to enlighten us.

"It is difficult to preserve life, but easy to find death. Still, no one would think of simply waiting for death, which comes so easily, just because it is difficult to preserve life.

"You value good behavior and virtuosity in order to stand out from other people. You obstruct your feelings and true nature by striving for this glory. To us, this seems worse than death.

"The only thing we are worried about is fulfilling our desires too soon. We worry that seeing too many beautiful women and eating too much excellent food might stop us from pursuing what we love. We worry that we may be too weak physically to enjoy being with beautiful women, or that our stomachs may be too full to eat any more delicious food.

"We have no time to waste worrying about our reputations or the state of our minds. For you to come and bother us simply because you are good at ruling people, for you to try and charm us with promises of fame and advancement, is shameful and terrible.

"But we will answer your question anyway.

"Listen. Just because someone knows how to regulate external things doesn't mean those things will become regulated. Furthermore, that person's body will still have to work and labor. However, if someone knows how to regulate internal things, he may actually succeed in regulating those things. His mind will then be at peace, and he can rest.

"Your method for regulating external things works on a temporary basis, and only for a single kingdom, at that. Furthermore, it is not harmonious with the human heart. Our method for regulating internals things can be applied throughout the whole universe. Furthermore, it would eliminate the need for princes and ministers.

"We always wanted to explain our doctrine to you. Now, we would like you to explain your doctrine to us."

Tse-Chan was bewildered, and found no answer for his brothers.

He later met Teng-hsi and told him what had happened.

"You are living with real men," said Teng-hsi, "and did not know it.

"Who says you are wise? Cheng has been governed all this time by chance, and not due to any skill of yours."

Chapter 10

The Joyous Life of Tuan-Mu-Shu

Tuan-Mu-Shu of Wei was a descendent from Tse-Kung.

He received an inheritance of ten thousand gold pieces. Untroubled by fate, he did whatever he wanted.

He lived a good life and indulged in his desires. With walls and buildings, pavilions and verandahs, gardens and parks, ponds and lakes, wine and food, vehicles and clothing, women and servants, he imitated the luxurious lifestyle of the princes of Chi and Chu.

Whenever he wanted something, he would go to any length to get it, no matter what the cost, or how difficult it was to achieve. He would even travel to faraway lands outside of the kingdom of Chi to find what his heart desired, to hear what his ear wanted to hear, to see what his eye wanted to see, to taste what his mouth wanted to taste.

Although such journeys may be difficult and dangerous, over mountains, across rivers, and down long roads, he would embark upon them as lightly as other men walk a few steps.

Every day, he entertained a hundred guests in his palace. There was always something cooking in his kitchens, and the halls and courtyards of his home were always filled with music and song. He distributed leftovers from his table first among his own family. What was left, he divided among his neighbors. Anything left after that was distributed throughout the kingdom.

Tuan-mu-Shu's mind and body began to deteriorate when he was sixty years old. He gave away his household and all of his treasures. He gave away precious stones, vehicles, clothing, women and servants. Within a year, he had given away all of his fortune, leaving nothing for himself or his children. When he became sick, he could not afford to buy medicine or a lancet, a sharp, often double-edged surgical instrument used to make small incisions. When he died, he did not even have enough money to pay for a funeral. His neighbors, who had benefited from him for many years, donated money to bury him. They gave the money he had given away back to his descendants.

When Ch'in-ku-li[10] heard this story, he said:

"Tuan-mu-Shu was a fool who brought disgrace to his ancestor."

When Tuan-Kan-Sheng heard this story, he said:

"Tuan-mu-Shu was a wise man. His virtue was greater than that of his ancestors. Rational people may have been surprised by his behavior, but he followed the right doctrine. The superior men of Wei only paid attention to proper behavior. There is no doubt that they didn't have a heart like his."

Chapter 11

The Foolishness of Wanting a Long Life

Meng-sun-Yang asked Yang Chu:

"Some people nurture life, taking care of their bodies as though they wish to live forever. Is that possible?"

"According to the laws of nature, there is no such thing as immortality," replied Yang Chu.

"But is it possible to have a very long life?" asked Meng-sun-Yang.

"According to nature," said Yang Chu, "there is no such thing as a very long life. Furthermore, life cannot be preserved by nurturing it, and the body does not benefit from taking care of it."

"What is long life then?" asked Meng-sun-Yang.

"In a long life, everything would be the same as it is now. In the past, the five good and bad passions were the same as they are now. In the past, the safety and danger of the four limbs were the same as they are now. Grief and joy were also the same, as was the constant fluctuation between peace and war. Having experienced all of these things, one would be quite tired at the age of one hundred. One would be even more tired if one lived a very long life!"

"If that's the case," said Meng-sun-Yang, "then perhaps a sudden death is better than a long life. Maybe to achieve what the heart desires, we should commit suicide by running onto a sword or jumping into deep water."

"No," said Yang Chu. "Once you have acquired life, do not pay any attention to it and simply allow it to occur. Take note of its desires and wishes, and in this manner wait for death.

"When death comes, do not pay attention to it. Let it simply arrive. Take note of what it brings you, and allow yourself to be taken away to nothingness.

"If you pay no attention to life or death, if you let them be as they are, then how can you be anxious about whether life will end too soon?"

Chapter 12

Self-Sacrifice and Self-Aggrandizement

Yang Chu said:

"Po-chêng-tse-kao[11] would not give up a hair of his body to help another person. He left his country and became a laborer. Yü the Great[12] did not care for his own body, which became quite emaciated.

"If the Ancients could have helped the world by hurting a hair on their own heads, they would not have done it. And, if the universe had been offered to a single person, he would not have accepted it.

"Because nobody would damage a single hair, and because nobody would do anything to help the world, the world was in a perfect state."

Ch'in-Tse asked Yang Chu:

"If you could, would you help humanity by pulling out a hair from your body?"

"Surely humanity is not helped by a single hair," answered Yang Chu.

"But if it were possible, would you do it?" asked Ch'in-Tse.

Yang Chu didn't answer.

Ch'in-Tse told this to Meng-sun-Yang, who replied:

"I will explain the Master's meaning.
"If you were offered ten thousand gold pieces for tearing off a piece of your skin, would you do it?"
"Yes, I would do it," replied Ch'in-Tse.

Then Meng sun Yang asked:

"Suppose you would get a kingdom for cutting off one of your limbs, would you do it?"

Ch'in-Tse did not answer.

"See now," said Meng-sun-Yang. "Compared with the skin, a single hair is unimportant. Compared with a limb, the skin is unimportant.
"However, many hairs together form skin, and many skins together form a limb. Therefore, even though a hair is just one of the many cells that compose the body, it should not be taken lightly."
"I don't know what to say," replied Ch'in-Tse. "If I asked Lao tse and Kuan Yin[13], they would agree with

your opinion. The Great Yü and Me ti would also agree with you."

Following this reply, Meng-sun-Yang turned back to his disciples and spoke of something else.

Chapter 13

The Vanity of Reputation

Yang Chu said:

"The world praises Shun-Yu, the Duke of Chow, and Confucius. The world condemns Chieh and Chow. Shun had to work hard. He ploughed in Ho yang and burned tiles in Lei tse. His body had no rest, and he knew nothing about rich food or warm clothing.

"His parents and relatives did not love him. His brothers and sisters showed him no affection.

"When he was thirty years old, he was forced to marry without telling his parents.

"When Yao gave him his empire to rule, Shun was already an old man, and his mind was declining. He knew his son Shang-Chun had no ability to rule, and so he left his empire to Yü. Still, Shun had to work and slave until he died.

"Of all people, Shun was the most pitiable and miserable.

"Shun put Kun to death on Mount Yu Shan, because he felt Kun's efforts to control the water and build an embankment were impracticable.

"Kun's son Yü followed in his father's footsteps. Although working for his enemy, he invested all of his energy on building the embankment. He was so busy that when a son was born to him, he did not have the time to hold it in his arms. He was so busy that when he walked by his own house, he did not have the time to enter. His body became withered and his hands and feet became hard due to his hard work. When Shun left his empire to Yü, he still lived in a small house. He wore only an elegant sash and a small crown. He had to work and slave until he died.

"Of all people, Yü was the most overworked and exhausted.

"When King Yü died, Cheng was still young, and the Duke of Chow became Prince Regent.

"The Duke of Chow was not content, and spread evil rumors about Chow throughout the empire. Chow stayed in the east for three years. He caused his older brother to be beheaded and his younger brother to be banished. As for himself, he was nearly killed as well. He had to work and slave until he died.

"Of all people, he was the most threatened and frightened.

"Confucius was very familiar with the old emperors and their doctrines. He even accepted invitations from the princes of his time. Still, when he was in Sung, the tree under which he was teaching his pupils was deliberately cut down. He was driven out of Wei, and his footprints were erased. He got into trouble in Shang and Chow and was beaten in Chen and Tsai. He was humiliated by Chi and insulted by Yang-hu. He had to work and slave until he died.

"Of all people, he was the most harassed and worried.

"All of these sages did not enjoy a single day of pleasure while they lived. After they died, their reputation has lasted for many years.

"But reputation cannot restore life.

"You given them praise, but they don't know it. You honor them, but they don't know it either. Now, there is no difference between these sages and a lump of earth.

"Chieh used up the wealth acquired by many generations. He achieved honor by conquering lands to the south. His was wise enough to control many subjects. He was strong enough to shake the land surrounded by the four seas. He indulged in whatever pleased his eyes and ears. He fulfilled every one of his heart's desires. He was happy and merry until he died.

"Of all people, he was the most irresponsible and wasteful.

"Chow also helped himself to the wealth of many generations, and became King.

"Everything submitted to his will.

"All night long, he gave himself up to his desires.

He indulged in lustful behavior with his concubines. He didn't make his life bitter by concerning himself with proper behavior or virtuosity.

"He was happy and merry until he was put to death.

"Of all people, he was the most immoral and excessive.

"These two villains enjoyed themselves while they lived, following their inclinations and fulfilling their desires. After they died, they were called fools and tyrants. But reality cannot be affected by reputations.

"Oblivious to criticism and unaware of praise, they were no different from a tree stump or a lump of earth.

"The four sages were widely admired, but they were troubled all of their lives. Equally and alike, they were all doomed to die at the end.

"The two villains were widely hated and despised, but they enjoyed themselves all of their lives. They too were doomed to die at the end."

Chapter 14

Difficulty and Ease of Government

Yang Chu had an audience with the King of Leang.

"To govern the world is as easy as turning around the palm of the hand," said Yang Chu.

"You have a wife and a concubine," said the King of Leang, "but you are unable to govern them. You have a three-acre garden, but you are unable to care for it. How then can you say that governing the world is like turning around the palm of your hand?"

"Look at the shepherds, your Majesty," answered Yang Chu. "A young boy, only five feet high, has the responsibility of carrying a whip and driving a hundred sheep. The boy wants them to go eastward, and they obey him. The boy wants them to go westward, and they obey him. Now let Yao drag a sheep, and Shen follow with a whip, and they will never move forward a yard. Fish that swallow ships do not enter small rivers.

"Wild geese that fly high in the sky do not land

on low marshes. Instead, they pass over the marshes as they fly. The notes C and Cis are not in harmony with quick and lively airs, because their sound is too different. Similarly, a man who is busy with important issues does not trouble himself with trivial ones. And a man who accomplishes great deeds does not accomplish small ones. That is what I meant."

Chapter 15

All Things Pass

Yang Chu said:

"Things that occurred in the most ancient times have faded from memory. Who remembers such things? A few things are preserved from the time of the three generations of Emperors[14], but the rest has been lost. A little is still known about the five rulers[15], but the rest is only presumed. Regarding the time of the three emperors[16], some events are hidden in obscurity and some are clear, but out of one hundred thousand events, not a single one is remembered. In our present life, some things are heard and some things are seen, but not even one out of ten thousand events is remembered. It is impossible to figure out the number of years that has passed since ancient times until the present day. Even if we just count from Fw-hsi onwards there are more than three hundred thousand years.

"In the end, everything is effaced. Every trace of intelligent and stupid men, of the beautiful and ugly, of the successful and failed, of the right and wrong, is obliterated. The only variable is whether the effacement occurs quickly or slowly.

"If anybody worries about the blame or praise that takes place in a single hour, so much so that he tortures his spirit and body, so much so that he struggles to make a name that will last some hundred years after his death—can the halo of fame give life to his dead bones, or return to him the joy of living?"

Chapter 16

The Nature of Man

Yang Chu said:

"Men are like the heaven and the earth. They cherish five virtues[17]. Of all creatures on the earth, man has the most skills. He cannot sustain and shelter himself using only his nails and teeth. He cannot defend himself using only his skin and muscles. By running, he cannot earn a living or escape danger. He does not have hair or feathers to protect him from the cold or the heat. Man must use other things to take care of his person. He must rely on his intelligence; brute force is not enough. Man values intelligence because it saves us, and despises brute force because it impinges on things.

"I do not really own my own body. When I am born, I must complete it. Furthermore, I don't really possess objects. Though I may have them now, I must part with them later. The body is necessary for being born, but things are necessary for maintaining the body.

"If a body were born complete, I could not possess

it. Also, I could not possess things that were not to be parted with in the future. It would be unlawful to possess a body or an object that actually belonged to the whole universe. No sage would take possession of things that actually belong to the universe.

"The perfect man is he who regards the body, and the things of the universe, as belonging to the universe.

"That is the highest degree of perfection."

Chapter 17

The Four Chimeras*

Yang Chu said:

"There are four things which do not allow people to rest:

"Long life. Reputation. Status. Wealth.

"Those who have these fourth things fear dead men and living men, power and punishment. They are always fugitives. Whether they are killed or whether they live, they spend their lives being controlled by external forces.

"People who do not try to live in defiance of the natural life do not desire a long life. Those who are not fond of honor do not want reputation.

"Those who do not want power do not want status.

"Those who are not greedy do not want to acquire wealth.

"It can truthfully be said that this type of man lives in accordance with his nature. In all of the world, he is unique.

"He regulates his life according to internal things.

"There is an old proverb which says: Man would be free from half of his desires if he were not married, and did not have an official career. If man could live without clothes and food, there would be no need for rulers or being ruled."

* A chimera is something that is impossible to achieve.

Chapter 18

All Pleasures are Relative

In the time of Chow, there was a well-known saying:

"Can a farmer sit down and rest?

"At dawn he heads for the field, and at night he returns.

"He considers this the constant course of human nature.

"He eats plain food that seems delicious to him. His skin and joints are rough and bloated, and his muscles and joints are thick and swollen. If he could spend one day wearing smooth fur, living in a silk tent, and eating fine food such as meat, millet, orchids, and oranges, he would become sick in his heart. His body would grow weak, and the fire in his soul would cause him to become ill.

"On the other hand, if the Prince of Shang or Lu tried to work in the field like a farmer for one day, they would soon be totally exhausted. Nevertheless, both of these men say that there is nothing better than their comforts and pleasures in this world.

"There was an old farmer in Sung who only wore rough clothes made from hemp. Even in the cold of winter, these were the only clothes he wore. When he worked in the fields in the spring, he allowed the sun to shine on his bare back, warming his body.

"He did not know that things such as large mansions and winter apartments, fine material and silk, fox and badger fur existed in the world.

"One day, he turned to his wife and said: 'People do not know how pleasant it is to have warm sunshine on the bare back. I will tell our prince about this. I am sure he will send me a fine present.'

"A rich man in the village said to the old farmer: 'There was once a man who enjoyed eating big beans, the fibrous stalk of the hemp plant, pungent-tasting cress, and duckweed, a plant that grows on stagnant water. He told the village elder of these foods. The elder tasted them, and they burnt his mouth and gave him a stomach ache.

"Everybody laughed and was angry with the old farmer. The old farmer was very ashamed.

"You resemble this man."

Chapter 19

The Wisdom of Contentment

Yang Chu said:

"How can a person who has the following four things—a comfortable house, fine clothes, good food, and pretty women—want anything else? A man who wants more will never be satisfied, and the inability to be satisfied is a worm that eats the body and mind.

"A ruler is not put to ease by loyalty. Indeed, loyalty may endanger one's body. Virtuosity cannot help the world. Indeed, it may harm one's life. Loyalty will not bring peace to a ruler, and the reputation of the loyal dwindles to nothing over time. The world does not benefit from virtuosity, and the reputation of the virtuous is worthless.

"How can rulers and subjects both be at ease? How can the world and the individual be helped at the same time? This is described in a saying of the Ancients."

Yu Tse[18] said:

"A man who rejects fame will have no sorrow."

Lao Tse said:

"Fame comes after reality. Nowadays, people pursue fame with great frenzy—is it not true that fame comes naturally if no attention is paid to it? Currently, fame means being looked up to and respected. The lack of fame means being humble and disgraced. Ease and pleasure come after honor and respect. Sorrow and grief accompany humbleness and disgrace. They are also in opposition to human nature. Ease and pleasure are harmonious with human nature. These things have reality."

Footnotes

¹ *Kuan Chang died in 645 BCE.*

² *Tien became King of Ch'i 370 BCE.*

³ *Po Yo and Shu-Ch'i were the sons of Prince Ku-Chu. When the prince died, he appointed Shu-Ch'i, the younger brother, to be his successor. Shu-Ch'i didn't want to take the position from his elder brother Po Yo, so he declined. Po Yo, who didn't want to act against his father's will, also declined the position. Both brothers left the area and died in poverty.*

⁴ *Yao and Shun were legendary leaders in ancient China. They were often revered as perfect kings who demonstrated kindness and diligence, and served as models for future Chinese rulers.*

⁵ *Chan-Chi was an official in the state of Lu who was famous for his ability to refrain from sex. For this reason, he did not father any children, thereby causing his family to shrink. His proper name was Fui-hsai-hui.*

⁶ *Tse Hung was a disciple of Confucius.*

⁷ Yen-Ping-Chung and Kuan-Yi-Wu were famous statesmen who served the dukes of Chi.

⁸ Tse-han was a famous minister of Cheng who lived in 550 BCE.

⁹ Nine degrees of relationship are counted, from great-great-grandfather to great-great-grandson.

¹⁰ Ch'in-ku-li was probably a pupil of the philosopher Me Ti.

¹¹ Po-chêng-tse-kao was a Taoist who lived during the time of Yao.

¹² Yü the Great controlled the great flood of the Yellow River. He was so occupied with this task that he forgot his own needs.

¹³ Kuan-Yin is a Tao philosopher.

¹⁴ The three generations of Emperors are the Emperors of Heaven, the Emperors of Earth, and the Human Emperors. They form what is known as the first fabulous epoch of Chinese history.

¹⁵ The five rulers are Fw-his, Shen-nung, Huang-ti, Yao and Shun.

¹⁶ *The three emperors are Yü, T'eng and Wen-Wang. They founded the first three dynasties.*

¹⁷ *Man's moral life is based on five virtues: kindness, honesty, proper behavior, knowledge, and trustworthiness.*

¹⁸ *Yu Tse is a philosopher who is believed to have lived in 1250 BCE.*